BRIAN JOHNSTON

Spiritual Realities

Are We Blind to Them?

Contents

1

Being Dead in Sins

I want to anchor our studies in this book in the narrative of 2 Kings chapter 6. We don't need a lot of background to this story; I simply want to let the relevant part of this narrative speak for itself. It concerns the man of God, Elisha, and his servant. And the setting of the episode we're interested in is at a time when the enemy king of Syria has sent an army to capture Elisha, the Israelite prophet and notable man of God. The Bible historian says…

"… he sent horses and chariots and a substantial army there, and they came by night and surrounded the city. Now when the attendant of the man of God had risen early and gone out, behold, an army with horses and chariots was circling the city. And his servant said to him, "This is hopeless, my master! What are we to do?" And he said, "Do not be afraid, for those who are with us are greater than those who are with them." Then Elisha prayed and said, "LORD, please, open his eyes so that he may see." And the LORD opened the servant's eyes, and he saw; and

behold, the mountain was full of horses and chariots of fire all around Elisha" (2 Kings 6:14-17).

Ever heard the saying that says: "one person with God is a majority"? Well, this is a classic example of how true that is. Let's recap on the specific details from our reading. In the morning, Elisha's servant looks out and sees the enemy army come to take them prisoner and, naturally enough, he's afraid. But the man of God at his side, Elisha, is totally unfazed by the same sight. And why is that? The reason is that he could see something that his servant couldn't see. He then prayed that his servant's eyes would be opened. The Lord answered this prayer, and suddenly the servant was also able to see God's protective army all around them: with chariots and horses of fire. Now he could understand how the prophet could be so calm and stress-free!

This reminds me of David's words at the beginning of Psalm 27. There, he expresses his own trust in God. He said that even if an army would surround him, and even though war should break out against him, he'd still be confident in God, in the God whom he trusted. That's the same as Elisha's experience. And now let's ask the question that we'll often find ourselves asking throughout this book: "What spiritual realities are we blind to?" It was certainly Paul's prayer for believers in the Church of God at Ephesus that the eyes of their heart might be enlightened (Ephesians 1:18) - in other words, that they might no longer be blind to spiritual realities. And those were the spiritual realities he was going to unfold to them in the writing of that letter. Paul's prayer "Open their eyes, Lord," was like the preacher's opening prayer before he begins his message. In Paul's prayer, he asks the Lord to grant receptiveness to his audience for the things he's going to reveal to them in the chapters that follow.

Let's begin our study with the very first spiritual reality a person needs to be made aware of. We'll take our reading now from the Old Testament prophet, Ezekiel, from the thirty-seventh chapter, the one that's made famous by its description of the so-called "valley of dry bones":

"The hand of the LORD was upon me, and He brought me out by the Spirit of the LORD and set me down in the middle of the valley; and it was full of bones. He had me pass among them all around, and behold, there were very many on the surface of the valley; and behold, they were very dry. Then He said to me, 'Son of man, can these bones live?' And I answered, 'Lord GOD, You Yourself know.' Again He said to me, 'Prophesy over these bones and say to them, "You dry bones, hear the word of the LORD." This is what the Lord GOD says to these bones: "Behold, I am going to make breath enter you so that you may come to life. And I will attach tendons to you, make flesh grow back on you, cover you with skin, and put breath in you so that you may come to life; and you will know that I am the LORD."'"

So I prophesied as I was commanded; and as I prophesied, there was a loud noise, and behold, a rattling; and the bones came together, bone to its bone. And I looked, and behold, tendons were on them, and flesh grew and skin covered them; but there was no breath in them. Then He said to me, "Prophesy to the breath, prophesy, son of man, and say to the breath, 'The Lord GOD says this: "Come from the four winds, breath, and breathe on these slain, so that they come to life."' So I prophesied as He commanded me, and the breath entered them, and they came to life and stood on their feet, an exceedingly great army. Then He said to me, 'Son of man, these bones are the entire house of Israel; behold, they say, "Our bones are dried up and our hope has perished. We are completely cut off."

Therefore prophesy and say to them, 'This is what the Lord GOD says: "Behold, I am going to open your graves and cause you to come up out of your graves, My people; and I will bring you into the land of Israel. Then you will know that I am the LORD, when I have opened your graves and caused you to come up out of your graves, My people. And I will put My Spirit within you and you will come to life, and I will place you on your own land. Then you will know that I, the LORD, have spoken and done it," declares the LORD'" (Ezekiel 37:1-14).

In these verses, the Lord in his Word graphically predicts that the nation of Israel will one day be revived before God. God's Spirit will one day breathe new life into Israel as a nation. It's pictured as if scattered bones on a valley floor are brought together. Then in turn tendons, flesh, and skin clothe them. Finally, the breath of life is breathed into them. But this is no Frankenstein creation of human imagination. This is a work of God. And it's the same when we as individuals come to faith in Christ in this period of God's grace. There can be no new life – no new birth experience – without it being the work of God in its entirety.

I remember in January 2004 - while in the Philippines - reading in the Philippine Inquirer newspaper about a moratorium on drug dealers. As a result of an appeal by the Pope, their death sentence was postponed. The newspaper described those on "Death Row" who were waiting for their fate to be determined as being "the living dead of the Philippines." Some newspaper headlines are very effective; that was one, because I've never forgotten it.

But here's the point - we're all "the living dead" in God's sight because of our sins. That's our natural condition until we come to Christ – we are *dead in our sins* (see Ephesians 2:1) – and that's why we can't even begin to hope that God will be pleased by our own good works and let us into heaven. A dead person cannot in any way contribute to his or her resurrection to new life. Being dead, he or she is powerless. Everything that must happen for a sinner to become acceptable to God depends on God – entirely upon God.

But you say: "Did I not repent?" "And was it not I who exercised faith?" Well, the Bible plainly teaches us that repentance (Acts 11:18) and faith (Philippians 1:29) are each granted by God in the first place. They only become ours (e.g. Matthew 9:22) after having been given to us by God. We were dead in God's estimation, remember? Not only can a dead patient not take any medicine for their healing; neither can any who are dead in sins improve themselves by taking the medicine of religion. Even repenting and believing is quite beyond them. They're dead after all. *"Salvation is of the Lord,"* as Jonah put it (Jonah 2:9). Salvation is wholly God's work from start to finish. Or as someone once said: "all we can contribute are our sins."

Like Israel on the banks of the Red Sea, we stand still and see the salvation of God. God destroyed the pursuing Egyptian army at that time. The Israelites didn't need to lift a hand to help themselves; God's outstretched hand performed all the work from start to finish. And it's the very same with us. God first breathes new life into us. Now no longer dead, we are then able to act in the repentance and faith it has pleased him to give us. Salvation is all of God. It's an insult to God's glory if we think that the work of faith was our own work foreseen by God from the start. It was, and is always, God working in us both to will and to work. If we think differently, it's only because we've failed to register how totally corrupted our human nature was through sin. There was not one vestige of good left in us: no part of our being that wasn't tainted with sin. We were utterly helpless – exactly in the same way a totally dead person is. This is straightforward Bible language. God doesn't reward our own faith with his salvation. We don't earn or merit any concessions by our repentance. It's by the grace of God that we're saved. It's one hundred percent by God's grace.

Ephesians chapter 2, when we come down to verse 5, tells us that what happened first was that we were *"quickened."* That's old and obsolete wording now in the English language. It simply means God made us alive. It obviously wasn't something we did ourselves. It happened to us. This underlines the point we're making – that the very first thing that happened in our experience of the saving grace of God was that he made us alive. The initiative and the initial action were both his.

Whether it's an eye-opener for you or not, what we're seeing clearly in this first chapter is the spiritual reality that in our sinner state before a holy God we were totally corrupt and helpless (e.g. Romans 3:13-18; 5:6), until such time as God in his rich mercy and great love and saving grace – and by his own sovereign action – gave us new life in Christ. Salvation is from the LORD only. We praise him, and reserve not the slightest boast for ourselves.

2

United with Christ

In the Gospel by Luke, our Lord Jesus in resurrection opened the minds of his followers to understand the Scriptures (Luke 24:45). We read this after hearing the recorded testimony of two of them who were exclaiming to others about their wonderful conversation earlier that day with Jesus. At first, they had not realised that the stranger who had been talking with them had in fact been Jesus himself, now raised from the dead. They had simply been captivated by his explanation of the Old Testament. For they now realised their holy Writings had always been pointing to Jesus and that could only mean that his death on the cross had always been in God's plan. To say that this was a revelation to them would be an understatement! They said their eyes had been opened – not only to see Jesus as the great theme of the Old Testament, but also to recognise it was the resurrected Jesus who was the very one speaking with them and giving them this wonderful Bible teaching that had set their hearts on fire.

It's our prayer that, as we open our Bibles, the Holy Spirit of

God will open our eyes also - as well as our minds - in order to give us an understanding of any spiritual realities we've previously been blind to. For example, when we trusted Jesus as our Saviour many amazing things happened to us that we can only discover if we read and understand our Bibles. For example, early in Romans chapter 6, Paul tells us that *"we ... died to sin"* (v.2). A Christian, a born-again believer on Christ, is someone who has died! To confirm we're not misunderstanding Paul's intention, let's check with Colossians 3:3. Writing to the local church of God at Colosse, the Apostle says plainly once more: *"you have died and your life is hidden with Christ in God."* Moments before, in the first verse of that same chapter, Paul had already said: *"you have been raised up with Christ."*

It would be quite legitimate to take this as a definition of a true Christian. He or she is someone who has died and been raised in this biblical sense. But what does it mean? If we now return to chapter 6 of Romans, we find in verse 6 that Paul has this to say: *"our old self was crucified with him,"* that is with Christ. This very plainly connects our death experience at the point of our salvation with the cross where Jesus died.

The old hymn asks: "Were you there when they crucified my Lord?" Well, it turns out that we were! Perhaps not as the hymn writer envisaged it, but certainly as the Spirit of God reveals it to our minds in the Bible. Every believer is associated with the crucifixion of Jesus. It's God who makes that definite association in his Word, the Bible. Everyone given by God to his son, everyone who comes to believe on the Lord Jesus, is seen as having died with Christ.

This is the spiritual reality we want to investigate in this chapter. Paul explains what it means for us to die to sin by stating that Christ himself died to sin. There must be a consistency between what it means for Christ to die to sin, and what it means for the Christian believer to die to sin – since both these expressions are found in the same place in our Bible. There's more than consistency in fact - there's **identification**. For the teaching that's at the back of the whole argument of Romans chapter 6 is the teaching of our union with Christ. Because of our union with Christ, what happened to him also happened to us.

Paul describes Christian believers' baptism as a likeness of Christ's death and resurrection. After our conversion, when we submit to this rite - that is the biblical ordinance of being totally dipped in water - it's in fact a public acknowledgement of our prior involvement in the death and resurrection of our Lord Jesus. So, more than identification, there's **involvement**. Paul reasons that if Christ died to sin, and we're identified with Christ, then it follows that we, too, died to sin – and as a practical consequence it would be out of place for us to now lead a life dominated by sinful practices.

That's the sense of the flow of this paragraph in our Bibles. And it's in support of the reality that we've been identified with Christ that Paul shares two things: a revelation of what happened at our conversion, and the clearest explanation possible of the meaning of our water baptism. These two things are linked by this thought that we're in union with Christ. It's at salvation, when by God's grace we're saved through faith, that we're identified with the Christ of the cross in his death and resurrection. When we believe, it's as if Christ's death becomes our death and it's then that we receive new life in Christ.

We're guaranteed never to face God's judgment for our sins simply because Jesus Christ served our sentence when dying on the cross. God reckoned that we were crucified with Christ when he died under our sentence of death, so it's all over and done with. And, of course, this covers all our sins in the future as well as our past sins as far as we're concerned. God doesn't make the same distinction between past and present as we do. He sees the end from the beginning. The whole landscape of time is always before God. God doesn't want us to remain blind to the security we have in our guaranteed salvation.

If you're someone who struggles with this teaching of the believer's eternal security in Christ, may I gently urge you to meditate on the Bible's presentation regarding our union with Christ? This lies at the root of any difficulty we may have in seeing our salvation as being for ever assured through Christ's death. If you struggle with that, might I suggest you've not yet seen clearly enough this amazing spiritual reality of our union with Christ? And it is truly amazing! The words of John 14:20 are stunning. Here's what that verse says: *"On that day you will know that I am in My Father, and you are in Me, and I in you."*

Jesus has been saying quite repeatedly that he's in the Father and the Father is in him. That's the union of the son with the father (see also John 10:38; 14:10,11; 17:21). But then he adds that we are in him and he is in each of us. Take time to absorb that. Each of us is one with Christ – and this is being said in the same way that he's one with the Father! That's why I say again that if you struggle with the idea of the believer's eternal security in Christ, may I ask you to reflect seriously on the spiritual reality of our union with Christ? It's only blindness to this that stops us seeing our salvation as being for ever assured through Christ's death.

Later, in water baptism we demonstrate that fact by "acting it out" – i.e, being buried in water and rising up from it again. Water baptism is only a symbolic witness to all who watch it taking place that we're testifying to the faith that's already saved us – so our water baptism is in effect a drama about our previous identification, and prior involvement, with a crucified and resurrected saviour.

We say again: Paul reasons here that, if Christ died to sin, and we're identified with Christ, then it follows that we, too, died to sin – and as a practical consequence it would be inappropriate for us to lead a life dominated by sinful practices now. This is Paul's answer to critics who were saying that if a Christian believer has had all of his or her sins forgiven then why don't they live as they please? Paul says the true preaching of salvation should never be misconstrued as a licence to keep on sinning.

The absolute bottom line of the apostle Paul's magnificent argument which we know as Romans chapter 6 can be simply stated as this: "you are not the person you once were, therefore don't live as you once lived." We're not the same person as we once were simply because we've died and now have a new life to live in a new way – not for human lusts but for God's glory. When our eyes are opened to the reality that we as believers are in union with Christ, this has massive implications for how we appreciate our salvation - and our water baptism - as well as giving us the Christian motivation to live well.

As a final thought, we may take this even further. In Christ's prayer recorded in John 17, he prays for his followers to become sanctified in truth (v.19) that they may be one with each other; but then he also prays that they also, altogether as God's gathered people, may be one with the triune God (vv.21,23,26). What another eye-opener that is! May God open our eyes and minds as disciples to the mind-blowing truths of the Bible!

3

Chosen from Eternity

There's an old hymn which encourages us to "count our blessings" and "name them one by one." We can start to do that – and it's good that we do – but we'll surely never get to the end of them for we've been blessed with every spiritual blessing in the heavenly realms in Christ – and do you think we could ever fathom that wealth of blessing? Paul says:

"Blessed be the God and Father of our Lord Jesus Christ, who has blessed us with every spiritual blessing in the heavenly places in Christ, just as He chose us in Him before the foundation of the world, that we would be holy and blameless before Him. In love He predestined us to adoption as sons and daughters through Jesus Christ to Himself, according to the good pleasure of His will, to the praise of the glory of His grace, with which He favored us in the Beloved. In Him we have redemption through His blood, the forgiveness of our wrongdoings, according to the riches of His grace which He lavished on us. In all wisdom and insight He made known to us the mystery of

His will, according to His good pleasure which He set forth in Him, regarding His plan of the fullness of the times, to bring all things together in Christ, things in the heavens and things on the earth.

In Him we also have obtained an inheritance, having been predestined according to the purpose of Him who works all things in accordance with the plan of His will, to the end that we who were the first to hope in the Christ would be to the praise of His glory. In Him, you also, after listening to the message of truth, the gospel of your salvation—having also believed, you were sealed in Him with the Holy Spirit of the promise, who is a first installment of our inheritance, in regard to the redemption of God's own possession, to the praise of His glory" (Ephesians 1:3-14).

That whole section – from Ephesians 1:3 down until verse 14 – is one continuous sentence in Paul's original letter, judging by the earliest copies we have. It's almost as if when Paul started to count, or rather list, all these blessings, he just couldn't stop!

Did you notice our reading was split into three parts by the use of the repeated expression *"to the praise of his glory"*? It's worth reflecting for a moment on these words that Paul repeats here. God has blessed us with this ultimate goal in view – that it should all be to the praise of his glorious grace. But just what does that mean? Praise, of course, is to give recognition: when we praise someone, we're recognizing his or her achievement. And the biblical word for glory seems to be associated with heaviness as reflected in Paul talking about the *"weight of* [God's] *glory"* (2 Corinthians 4).

This reminds me of how at times we recognize there are some people whose opinions *"carry weight."* In their field of endeavour, they are recognised as *"heavyweights."* Nothing carries more weight than the words and works of God. Nothing or no-one is more deserving of our recognition and gratitude. Well might we praise God for his truly weighty intervention in shaping our destiny!

The first part of this long list of blessings at the opening of Paul's letter to the Ephesians contains blessings which are attributed to God the Father. Basically, they centre around the fact that he chose us in the timeless, dateless past and lovingly predestined us to be his adopted sons and daughters. Well, if the first part of this long sentence of Paul's was about blessings we could attribute to the Father, the next part we read relates the blessings directly to Christ, the son. Such things as redemption, forgiveness and a wonderful inheritance feature prominently.

Finally, in the third instalment, the blessings are related to the actions of God the Spirit because we're reminded of the Spirit's work inasmuch as we've been sealed in him. The fact that the Holy Spirit is in us is presented here in terms of viewing him as being the guaranteeing deposit of all that's to come – a down payment in advance of everything else that's promised.

Of course, all the blessings in all three parts are all *"in Christ."* The Apostle Paul uses that little expression *"in Christ"* about eighty times in his Bible letters (81 times in the King James Version). Our new Christian identity should affect the way we view ourselves all the time. We're in Christ and Christ is in us as individual members of the Church that is his Body. Paul teaches on that in his letter to the Colossians, from chapter 1 and verse 23:

"Now I rejoice in my sufferings for your sake, and in my flesh I am supplementing what is lacking in Christ's afflictions in behalf of His body, which is the church. I was made a minister of this church according to the commission from God granted to me for your benefit, so that I might fully carry out the preaching of the word of God, that is, the mystery which had been hidden from the past ages and generations, but now has been revealed to His saints, to whom God willed to make known what the wealth of the glory of this mystery among the Gentiles is, the mystery that is Christ in you, the hope of glory. We proclaim Him ...

For I want you to know how great a struggle I have in your behalf and for those who are at Laodicea, and for all those who have not personally seen my face, that their hearts may be encouraged, having been knit together in love, and that they would attain to all the wealth that comes from the full assurance of understanding, resulting in a true knowledge of God's mystery, that is, Christ Himself, in whom are hidden all the treasures of wisdom and knowledge... For in Him all the fullness of Deity dwells in bodily form, and in Him you have been made complete, and He is the head over every ruler and authority; ...

And when you were dead in your wrongdoings and the uncircumcision of your flesh, He made you alive together with Him, having forgiven us all our wrongdoings, having canceled the certificate of debt consisting of decrees against us, which was hostile to us; and He has taken it out of the way, having nailed it to the cross. When He had disarmed the rulers and authorities, He made a public display of them, having triumphed over them through Him" (Colossians 1:24–2:15).

Notice that he talks about a *"mystery"* there. I want to suggest to you that there are in fact three mysteries there - all centred on the person of Christ of course – and perhaps really all aspects of the same *"mystery of Christ."* We're first introduced to **the Incorporated Christ** (1:24-26) with the talk of his *"Body"*; then to **the Indwelling Christ** (1:27) by mention of *"Christ in you the hope of glory"*; and finally we have **the Incarnate Christ** (2:2,3) brought before us as the one in whom all the fullness of deity came to reside bodily. Paul's prayer in that regard is about enthusing, uniting, and enriching their sure grasp of truly knowing the incarnate Christ.

In Christ alone are found all the treasures of wisdom (v.3); all the fullness of deity (v.9); all the supremacy of rule and authority (v.10); all the blessings of our salvation (vv.11-14); and all the triumphs of God's grace (v.15). These are all things revealed to us in this section of the Apostle Paul's writings. Of course, that's what a mystery means in the biblical sense. It's not a truth that's concealed from us, but a teaching that's now revealed to us. Previously hidden, but now made plain through the Scriptures and by the Spirit of God. God's biblical mysteries are, in effect, open secrets.

Let's conclude with a reference to what's been called the

"Golden Chain." It's found in Romans chapter 8 where Paul talks about those *"whom He predestined, He also called; and these whom He called, He also justified; and these whom He justified, He also glorified"* (Romans 8:30). That's an unbreakable chain spanning from eternity to eternity, starting out from the wonderful reality we began by considering: that of our having been chosen in Christ (Ephesians 1:4).

And there are four links in this unbreakable chain. This is God's plan for each Christian believer and it's one that gives confirmation of our eternal security in Christ. Those predestined are those who are called (*"the called"* - 1 Corinthians 1:24); and are again the very same as those who are justified; and also those who will be glorified. The same persons are in view at each stage. It's interesting to note that the final one, glorified, is set in the past tense although it clearly hasn't yet happened. That just goes to show that it's certain to happen, so much so that God treats it as already having taken place. That underlines the fact that no-one who begins this chain of events is going to fail to complete this four-stage journey. We're secure in Christ, from eternity to eternity. Not only is Christ to be glorified in us – that's remarkable – but we're to be glorified in Christ (2 Thessalonians 1:12) – and that's even more remarkable. It's the ultimate display of our sanctification. We'll then be as much like Christ as it's possible for created beings to be.

"All things" are to be given to those (the *"all"*) for whom Christ was delivered up (v.32). This refers back to all those already described as predestined, called, justified and glorified. Christ gave himself up for his Church (Ephesians 5:25). Only those who start off as having been given by the father to the son will

receive *"all things."* Christ's death will be fully effective for all those for whom it was intended to be so.

May God open our eyes to the profound teaching of the Bible that we were chosen by God in Christ from the dateless, timeless period before the universe existed. And the impact of all this teaching for the here and now is that we should no longer live the old life as the old self we once were in pre-conversion days (Galatians 2:20); but rather what comes with the change that God has brought about in us is the obligation to yield ourselves in the service of Christ (Romans 6:13; 12:1).

4

Members of Christ's Body

In 1 Corinthians chapter 2, the Apostle Paul is once again talking about insight into the purposes of God that can't be gained by any natural means. He talks of how the human eye can't see, nor the ear hear, nor the human mind ever understand, the things God has now provided for the Christian believer. He roots it there in an understanding of the cross where Christ died. And this insight can only be given through the Spirit of God. Paul argues that we don't know what each other is thinking. Only the human spirit of that same person knows that person's own thoughts.

This is obviously true. But Paul argues, amazingly, that we can know what God's thoughts are (even though we can't know what each other is thinking)! That's because each believer on Jesus Christ has been given God's Spirit to reside in him or her (Romans 8:9). As a result, we now discover a resistance to indulging the cravings we once had. By having the Spirit of God and of Christ, we have the mind of Christ. It's famously described in the Bible as the mindset that prioritises the needs of others above our own personal needs (Philippians 2:1-5). Such new thinking in a Christian convert is plain evidence that God's Spirit has taken up residence within.

Something else we could never be aware of by any natural means is the spiritual reality that each of us, as a believer on the Lord Jesus, is a member of an invisible Church grouping. Even if we should never frequent a place of Christian worship, we nevertheless belong to the Church Jesus himself spoke about when he declared that his mission was to build what he described as *"My church."* This church-building mission is described as God's eternal purpose (Ephesians 3:11).

When a person receives Christ as personal Saviour, he or she is invisibly baptised by Jesus in the Spirit and by that means becomes incorporated as a member of Christ's universal Church. This is yet another unseen reality to which our eyes are opened only when we read our Bible. Let's do that now by looking at 1 Corinthians chapter 12. But if we're going to understand this chapter correctly, we're first going to have to learn to distinguish between two uses of the same word for "church" that we come across in the New Testament.

We often hear people talking about "the early church" without defining what they mean. Judging by the context, they're most likely referring to "the first Christians." You may say I'm splitting hairs, but it has to be said that they are using the word "church" in a way that's not clearly defined in the New Testament. Sloppiness on our part with terminology which the Holy Spirit has used with precise accuracy has led to confused thinking over the centuries – this is why it's vital to strive for the accurate biblical use of the word translated as "church."

What, then, are the biblical meanings of this word church or - as it was in the original Greek language of the New Testament - *ekklesia*? There are basically two. We find it used of a well-defined group of Christian disciples in a given locality operating - under the care of elders and deacons - as those commissioned to carry out the functions of worship, prayer and witness. That's the first of the two meanings we encounter in the New Testament writings: in other words, being a local church in the biblical sense. However, it's also used with a different meaning. It's also used in the overall sense of all who have ever truly professed saving faith in Christ, beginning from the time of the first Spirit-filled preaching recorded in Acts chapter 2 until the future time referred to in 1 Thessalonians 4 (the so-called 'Rapture event') when Christ will return to the air to receive to himself – and so take away from the earth all Christians, whether dead or alive.

Although the Apostle Paul is writing to the local Church of God at Corinth throughout his two letters that are addressed to them, we find that in this particular chapter, the twelfth, he's largely taken up with teaching about the universal Church – if I may call it that, so long as we understand by that expression the body of all believers as we defined it biblically a moment ago.

> *"For even as the body is one and yet has many members, and all the members of the body, though they are many, are one body, so also is Christ. For [in] one Spirit we were all baptized into one body, whether Jews or Greeks,*

whether slaves or free, and we were all made to drink of one Spirit" (1 Corinthians 12:12-13).

Perhaps at this point it would be good to comment on two metaphors which the Bible uses to help us understand this yet another unseen spiritual reality – I'm talking about Christ's (universal) Church. To explain himself in this regard, God gives us the picture of human marriage, and the other picture he uses is our human body. It's mainly Ephesians chapter 5 that takes up the picture of marriage between a husband and a wife as illustrating the eternal relationship between the Lord Jesus Christ and all believers. It's amazing to consider the intimacy – this eternal intimacy – that God wants to have with us! The husband's love for his wife, and the wife's submissive respect for her husband, in a lifelong union was God's intention in giving us the institution of marriage – in order to show the respective roles of Christ and his Church.

More widely, and certainly here in 1 Corinthians 12, we come across the other metaphor which invites us to understand something of Christ's Church by analogy with the functioning of our own human body. Let's return to our reading at verse 14:

"For the body is not one member, but many. If the foot says, 'Because I am not a hand, I am not a part of the body,' it is not for this reason any the less a part of the body. And if the ear says, 'Because I am not an eye, I am not a part of the body,' it is not for this reason any the less a part of the body. If the whole body were an eye, where would the hearing be? If the whole were hearing, where

would the sense of smell be? But now God has placed the members, each one of them, in the body, just as He desired. If they were all one member, where would the body be? But now there are many members, but one body. And the eye cannot say to the hand, 'I have no need of you'; or again the head to the feet, 'I have no need of you.'

On the contrary, it is much truer that the members of the body which seem to be weaker are necessary; and those members of the body which we deem less honorable, on these we bestow more abundant honor, and our less presentable members become much more presentable, whereas our more presentable members have no need of it. But God has so composed the body, giving more abundant honor to that member which lacked, so that there may be no division in the body, but that the members may have the same care for one another. And if one member suffers, all the members suffer with it; if one member is honored, all the members rejoice with it" (1 Corinthians 12:14-26).

Throughout that entire section which we've just read (vv.14-26), Paul by the Spirit is dealing primarily with the human body. But the analogy is then clearly drawn in v.27 so that all the preceding points now have their point of application. It (v.27) says, *"Now you are Christ's body, and individually members of it."* Returning to our earlier distinction between the two major uses of the word "church" in the New Testament, we shouldn't be confused when Paul says to the believers at Corinth, that is, to the local gathered disciples in the Church of God at Corinth who were following - albeit imperfectly - the teaching of the Lord's Apostles: *"you are Christ's body."*

Obviously, those to whom this letter was addressed were not the whole universal Church! They were only a small subset, even at that time, of the body of all believers. The sense here must then be that what the entire Church is in its character was to be true of this – and every other – local church. Each and every Church of God in any given locality should aim to be true in its expressed character to the universal Church. More than that, the emphasis on Christian unity in this context requires that all local churches when functioning biblically should be harmoniously inter-dependent. It's evident that independent local churches practising different beliefs fall shamefully short of expressing the spiritual reality of the flawless union of all Christian believers in the universal Body of Christ. Each local church, each of them holy in character, and all these churches together functioning in a co-ordinated way, is the biblical – and surely only – adequate way of fulfilling this grand body metaphor of the universal Church.

5

Living Stones in God's House

Other than when the word "church" is used to describe all believers in Christ's Body, the other use of this same word in the New Testament is when it stands for a local gathering of disciples. For example, Paul begins his letters to the Corinthians by saying that he's writing to the Church of God at Corinth (1 Corinthians 1:1,2). There were, of course, local churches at other places too, such as Colosse, Philippi and, of course, at Jerusalem. On three occasions, we have a plural reference to *"the churches of God."* It's plain to see that those instances of the word are not referring to all believers universally in what we've already seen is biblically described by the metaphor of the Body of Christ (Ephesians 1:22,23). That, by contrast, is a unique church, by its very definition. And it's universal; whereas each local church had its own geographical limiter, being at Corinth or Jerusalem or at some other identified place. We can even readily check the observation that there was never more than a single church noted in any one identified place.

Coming back to the exact meaning of the word "church," we

also observe that its meaning is made clear by its use, in secular as well as religious settings. A single glance at a verse such as Acts 19:39 is all it should take to convince us that the essence of this word "church" is found in a gathering of persons who have been called out for a specific purpose. This remains true whether it's a gathering of secular protestors (as in Acts 19:39) or in the religious gatherings of those forming a local church in their designated physical location.

God's design of the local church (as something that meets together physically) was not dependent on the constraints of what was feasible at any historical moment in time. The corporate assembling together of people in time, in space and in a common purpose, is at the very heart of God's design for his local church. It isn't a preferential or variable feature. Only supporting features may be varied at different times, not the core essence of a thing.

The local church is a spiritually designated "place" where the presence of God can be experienced corporately by those assembled physically. This gives to it its temple identity (1 Corinthians 3:16,17 – something that cannot be "placeless") in a way that's consistent with the whole of Bible revelation. Even within the extended possibilities of the eternal state, God is described as tabernacling among those who are his own within city limits in a setting that suggests the most intimate appreciation of God's presence (Revelation 21).

But, let's be quite clear, the meaning of "church" in its biblical sense is never a physical building nor are believers said to "go to church." These are modern expressions that we'd have to say are a bit sloppy in departing from biblical exactness. What we're saying is that faithful believers who respond to Christ's teaching are those who themselves form the church. The physical place where they gather is simply a convenient meeting-place. It doesn't confer any sanctity whatsoever. The physical meeting-place could be a private house or it could be a rented community hall. In saying this, we come to another important Bible metaphor, and that's the one that describes each true born again believer in Christ as "a living stone." Let's check out the verse in 1 Peter 2:5 where we meet this idea:

"Coming to Him as to a living stone ... you also, as living stones, are being built up as a spiritual house for a holy priesthood, to offer spiritual sacrifices that are acceptable to God through Jesus Christ" (1 Peter 2:4,5).

A local church functions corporately by actually gathering for, as we said before, the essence of the word "church" is found in the assembling together of disciples, and that statement is supported by our text in Peter. Did you notice the introduction to it (in v.4) is about *"coming to"* or *"drawing near."* We know we come to Christ for salvation, once, on an individual basis; but this coming that Peter talks about is something that's collective and on-going, involving a drawing near together as gathered worshippers (on earth) for the offering up of spiritual sacrifices (in heaven). Some have stressed that this coming together may be thought of as a coming together in obedience to the teaching of the cornerstone. Others have also observed that the "drawing near" to Christ mentioned in these verses may be compared directly with the same kind of "drawing near" when the gathered tribes of Israelite worshippers congregated at the temple three times each year under the Old Covenant.

Certainly, in our verse from Peter, Christian disciples are viewed as assembling on earth so as to function as temple priests, as a priestly house in fact. And notice this: we draw near to Christ, the Living Stone (v.4) and where is he? He's the precious Cornerstone of God's House on earth that's been laid above in the Zion that's in heaven (v.6). Remember we said this verse is dealing with God's design for Christian worship? That's because it talks of a holy priesthood offering up spiritual sacrifices of praise. Living stones on earth drawing near to the Living Stone in heaven. This would indicate (and there's support for this elsewhere in the Hebrews letter) that the coming together and drawing near of the gathered people facilitates an experience that is simultaneously in two places at one time.

On the one hand, there's the gathering of the priestly house on earth for the purpose of drawing near to offer spiritual sacrifices. On the other hand, where we draw near to is the very sanctuary in heavenly Zion above where Christ is, exalted as the primary Living Stone and the exalted Cornerstone in God's House, and we draw near to him there. (The spiritual reality of what it means to be God's House can thus be seen to be bound up with this other spiritual reality of a gathered priesthood worshipping in heaven, see Hebrews 3:6; 6:19; 10:19).

Unless we're into architecture or the science of building structures, we may not have thought too much about exactly what a cornerstone was or is. Let's start with the seemingly obvious: there's strong Bible support for what seems to be, on the face of it, an obvious idea: a cornerstone was after all – "the stone at the corner." But things are rarely that simple. And this is no exception. Bible experts suggest there are two ideas that can satisfy the Bible use of the term "cornerstone." First of all, it could have been a foundation-stone upon which the structure of the building rested. Or, it might have referred in other instances to a topmost or capstone which linked the last tier of the two walls of a building together at the corner (International Standard Bible Encyclopaedia). In which case, it could be described as "the head of the corner." A Bible sourcebook with a good reputation agrees that "It would appear cornerstones were placed in different positions as regards elevation … a term equally applicable to the chief stone at the top and that in the foundation" (Unger).

We've seen when the apostle Peter was writing to New Testament believers, who would have been in local churches of God, he began at first by describing the Lord as a *"living stone"* before turning to his readers and saying: *"you also, as living stones, are being built up as a spiritual house for a holy priesthood, to offer spiritual sacrifices that are acceptable to God through Jesus Christ. For this is contained in Scripture: "BEHOLD, I AM LAYING IN ZION A CHOICE STONE, A PRECIOUS CORNERSTONE, AND THE ONE WHO BELIEVES IN HIM WILL NOT BE PUT TO SHAME"* (1 Peter 2:4-6).

If these believers, and churches, addressed by Peter were located throughout the five Roman Provinces he mentions, then, of course they must have been in a Christian unity, one in which they were linked together by Peter's colleagues in leadership – his fellow-elders as he calls them. This idea of

Christian unity might even be thought of, in a way, as being a result of Jesus being the Cornerstone of God's spiritual house. Because it follows that a cornerstone links – or unites – two walls of a building and so it links together the whole building simply from its position of being at the junction of two main walls. Yet another apostle, Paul, when he, too, talks of Jesus as the Cornerstone, goes on to say of him: *"in whom* [each] *building, being joined together, grows into a holy temple in the Lord"* (Ephesians 2:21). Paul was writing these words to the Church of God in Ephesus, setting them in context alongside all the other New Testament churches of God when he spoke of every (local) building, being joined together, growing into a holy temple in the Lord.

And so, in talking about God's building, his house, we're talking about a visible togetherness of believers – just like the first believers who were all linked together by their commitment to put into effect the New Testament pattern for Christian discipleship. That original pattern of discipleship was what Paul had described to his friends at Rome as the one mould of Christian teaching (Romans 6:17). Believers in all the churches of God had been poured into the same mould.

Now, one interesting feature of cornerstones noted by historians and archaeologists - and perpetuated until recent times - is that they were time capsules; that is, they contained artefacts from the time of building, often including the original building plan. Jesus as the Cornerstone is Jesus as he relates to the specific shape of our service. The pattern of our service is something that's precious to God and found in Christ, in his teaching given to the Apostles to pass on to us and preserved down the centuries for all generations of believers. How we're built up and built together with others in Christian testimony for the Lord is important to God. But judge that for yourself from Jesus' role as the cornerstone!

The Bible's use of this imagery – the metaphor of Jesus Christ as the cornerstone – is strongly associated with the human rejection of God's purposes (Matthew 21:33-45, 23:38). The Jewish nation rejected Jesus' claim to be their Messiah, and so God rejected the first century Jewish Temple. The Lord Jesus Christ is the cornerstone – he has the chief place – in God's replacement spiritual building, a building comprised of all who accept Jesus' claims, and who also obediently build their lives of discipleship on the pattern left for us in the New Testament Scriptures.

But let's ask again: "What is God's House?" The writer of the Hebrews' letter tells those for whom it was originally intended that they are God's House – in fact, linking himself with them, he says *"whose house we are"* – and then he adds the condition: *"if we hold fast ..."* (3:6) without *"falling away"* (see Hebrews 6:6). Now, let me say this very carefully: if to have a place in God's House means receiving Christ's salvation – and only that – then falling away from God's House can only mean losing that same salvation. But the Bible does NOT teach that we, once saved, can be lost again. No child can ever be unborn, and neither can any of God's spiritual children who have put their faith in Christ and been born again. And that makes God's House something to be distinguished from the vast company of all those who have known salvation by God's grace through personal faith in Jesus Christ, and is also to be distinguished even from all currently living believers.

The Hebrews' letter was written, as its name implies, to early Jewish Christians. They'd left behind the ceremonial Law of Moses to embrace Jesus as the Messiah. By following the Apostles' teaching they found themselves in the New Testament Churches of God. They were united in belief and practice (Acts 15). This is the spiritual reality of God's House on earth with believers as its living stones who gather together to draw near to worship God in heaven.

6

The Value of Knowing Christ

After 15 years of financing excavations in the Valley of the Kings with scarcely anything to show for his expenditure, Lord Carnarvon had begun to wonder if it would all prove fruitless. But then a telegram arrived. It was from Howard Carter, telling him to come to Luxor immediately. And so it was that, on 26 November 1922, Carter and Lord Carnarvon stood in front of the sealed door of Tutankhamun's tomb. First, Carter made a small hole in the door and then he inserted a candle. In answer to Carnarvon's anxious question, "Can you see anything?" Carter famously replied, "Yes, wonderful things."

When the Apostle Paul begins to write his letter to the Ephesians, he prays for them that they'd see wonderful things from what he was about to share with them. Here's his prayer: *that the God of our Lord Jesus Christ, the Father of glory, may give you a spirit of wisdom and of revelation in the knowledge of Him. I pray that the eyes of your heart may be enlightened, so that you will know what is the hope of His calling, what are the riches of the glory of His inheritance in the saints, and what is the boundless greatness of*

His power toward us who believe" (Ephesians 1:15-19).

The sense is, because they'd already been enlightened, Paul was praying that they would get to know God even more personally through coming to realize three facts: the hope of God's calling; the rich glory of God's inheritance and the surpassing greatness of God's power. What these things are is explained by what follows, especially in chapter two. As a preacher prays before he delivers his message, so that his audience may be helped to understand it, so Paul prays in the same way here. The content of his message in chapter two interprets for us the requests of his prayer back in chapter one.

Before we explore chapter two, it's perhaps worth observing that when Paul prays they will have a deeper knowledge of God (Ephesians 1:17), he's talking about the kind of knowledge that comes through experience. We're able to tell that because the Greek language distinguished this from the knowledge that came from observation. And, in fact, this particular word - as used here - conveys the sense of a more exact form of that type of experiential knowledge. Paul was directing his message to believers in the local Church of God at Ephesus, and he wants their evaluation of their place in that local church to flow from a greater appreciation of the Lord – one that gave an intelligent awareness of God's calling, inheritance and power. He begins to expand upon these as we come to chapter two:

> *"And you were dead in your offenses and sins, in which you*
> *previously walked according to the course of this world,*
> *according to the prince of the power of the air, of the spirit*
> *that is now working in the sons of disobedience. Among*

them we too all previously lived in the lusts of our flesh, indulging the desires of the flesh and of the mind, and were by nature children of wrath, just as the rest. But God, being rich in mercy, because of His great love with which He loved us, even when we were dead in our wrongdoings, made us alive together with Christ (by grace you have been saved), and raised us up with Him, and seated us with Him in the heavenly places in Christ Jesus, so that in the ages to come He might show the boundless riches of His grace in kindness toward us in Christ Jesus. For by grace you have been saved through faith; and this is not of yourselves, it is the gift of God; not a result of works, so that no one may boast. For we are His workmanship, created in Christ Jesus for good works, which God prepared beforehand so that we would walk in them.

Therefore remember that previously you, the Gentiles in the flesh, who are called 'Uncircumcision' by the so-called 'Circumcision' which is performed in the flesh by human hands— remember that you were at that time separate from Christ, excluded from the people of Israel, and strangers to the covenants of the promise, having no hope and without God in the world. But now in Christ Jesus you who previously were far away have been brought near by the blood of Christ. For He Himself is our peace, who made both groups into one and broke down the barrier of the dividing wall, by abolishing in His flesh the hostility, which is the Law composed of commandments expressed in ordinances, so that in Himself He might make the two one new person, in this way establishing peace; and that He might reconcile them both in one body to God through the cross, by it having put to death the hostility.

And He came and preached peace to you who were far away, and peace to those who were near; for through Him we both have our access in one Spirit to the Father. So then you are no longer strangers and foreigners, but you are fellow citizens with the saints, and are of God's household, having been built on the foundation of the apostles and prophets, Christ Jesus Himself being the cornerstone, in whom the whole [or every] building, being fitted together, is growing into a holy temple in the Lord, in whom you also are being built together into a dwelling of God in the Spirit" (Ephesians 2:1-22).

In other words, Paul calls on these believers to remember what they once were. They once were *"even as the rest"* of humanity, being once *"dead in* [their] *... sins."* *"But"* – and we thank God for that word! - Paul describes in some detail the tremendous changes brought about by God's grace. Notice how he mentions *"the heavenly places"* – one of 5 mentions in this letter of an expression that's found nowhere else in our Bibles. These believers were on the earth as far as their temporal existence was concerned, but at the same time they equally belonged to the eternal realm of reality – the realm described here as the heavenly places. Down here, we can distinguish between past, present and future – even as we make progress to become the person God wants us to be. But, in another sense, in the eternal realm, there's no distinction; the great spiritual realities are already in place now, as God sees them. It's revealed to us that we're raised and seated with Christ.

God's ultimate purpose is not our salvation, but rather that we should be something for him, for his glory. Previously, in Deuteronomy 32:9, God once said of his former people, Israel, that they were his "portion" and his "inheritance." Here in this chapter, Paul makes it clear that same racial barrier no longer applies. God is now, in this age, dealing with Gentiles on an equal footing with Jews. That's the difference the cross has made. Jews and Gentiles are fellow-members of the Church which is Christ's Body, which when viewed in the eternal or heavenly realm is complete and perfect. But we also see its members who are on earth – specifically those whom Paul is writing to in the Church of God at Ephesus – who are struggling to grasp what God intends them to become for him now. And Paul prays they'll grasp it.

Paul tells this Gentile local church that they're no longer separate from Christ, nor excluded from the promises, nor strangers with neither hope nor God. Far from it, they've actually been brought, he says, into *the household of God.* The word used there means either "family" or "house," and we must in every case find out which is the correct meaning from the immediate context. Here, since there's talk about building, and about a foundation and a cornerstone, Paul has to be referring to "the house" idea rather than "the family" of God in this instance.

Paul, at the end of chapter two, begins to elaborate on what God has in mind as the goal of our conversion experience in this life – it's for us to become a house or temple for God. Paul's no longer describing a scene in the eternal heavenly realms at this point; he's talking about something on earth – something that those in the Church of God in Ephesus were a part of. Paul never describes the whole universal Church the Body as being God's temple. For God's temple is capable of being destroyed (1 Corinthians 3:16,17) but that simply can't happen to the Body of Christ, as the Lord's famous words in Matthew 16 prove.

Many commentators simply assume Paul is talking about the Church the Body at the end of Ephesians chapter 2. This even has an impact on the translation of verse 21 – should it read "all the building" or should it say "every building" in relation to what's growing into a holy temple in the Lord? The point at dispute is the word "the" – is it properly there or not? More than half of the ancient manuscripts say "no" – and that leads respected authorities to say that the most accurate meaning here is "every building." That, in turn, means we're talking about an integrated structure on earth, spoken about as having a foundation and a cornerstone belonging to this single temple.

Obedient believers like those to whom Paul was writing – that is, in Gentile and Jewish local churches – are urged to visibly unite on earth so as to express the wonderful reality of Christ's universal Church. Sadly, we fail to do that when throughout Christendom we're divided by differences. The ending of Ephesians chapter 2 is looking at the Church the Body, not as it is in the heavenly realms, but as it is in its earthly expression.

For all believers today, enlightened from the time of their salvation, Paul's prayer applies. He's praying that we come to experience more of God personally and saying how it can happen. To see how is to travel to the end of this chapter with Paul and to be invited to belong to this temple made of people – people whom God is delighted to view today as his inheritance – in the same way as he once regarded Israel as being his inheritance. This is the hope God wants to realize now by calling us through the Gospel! It's part of the value of knowing Christ. Are our eyes open to this?

7

Meeting with God

An inspiring occasion is described for us in Nehemiah chapter 8. As the sermon was about to begin, the people stood up as one man in recognition of the fact that when God's Book is opened by the preacher it's God who speaks through his Word. The talk that was given by Ezra, who was the preacher on that occasion, must have been about the biblical command for God's Old Testament people to gather to observe their annual religious celebrations (or "Feasts"). We can say that judging by the reaction of the audience, for they reacted by confessing their failure to observe those particular gatherings (see Exodus 23; Leviticus 23; Deuteronomy 16). These were times when the people were to gather at the so-called Place of the Name (Deuteronomy 12:5).

The reference there is to the Name of God and the temple at Jerusalem. And it was precisely there at the Temple – and at those times that were fixed in Israel's annual calendar – that God's Old Testament people experienced the localised temple-dwelling presence of their omnipresent God. And on one occasion each year they even watched their high priestly representative head towards its innermost sanctuary, known as the holies.

Reading 1 Kings 9 recently, the following basic thought impressed itself on me: God was there perpetually in his temple (he explicitly said his Name, eyes and heart would be there "forever" or "perpetually"), but the tribes only actually *experienced* this fact when they assembled or came together there at the set feasts. At all other times during the year, they would have had no sense of this being the case while they were scattered from North to South and from East to West throughout their tribal territories. God was still there, of course, according to his faithful promise, but they themselves weren't there to experience it and testify to it.

Those Old Covenant set feasts we're talking about were part of the old order of Old Testament shadows or symbolic rituals that merely anticipated the substance of New Testament reality that was then still to come. It was precisely on those occasions, we say again, that the then people of God came together to experience the Temple-dwelling presence of God that was always localised at the temple, the place known as the Place where God had chosen to cause his Name, meaning his presence, to dwell.

Turning now to what this was prefiguring, we find that for followers of Christ, obeying New Testament teaching, the equivalent language - corresponding to those times when the tribes once gathered - is found whenever the Bible describes Christian disciples as "coming together as churches" (NASB).

This is language that may be viewed as restricted in its scope of application to what we find contextually alongside its four mentions in 1 Corinthians 11-14. On all the worship, prayer and Bible ministry occasions described in that section, the Temple-dwelling presence of God could be experienced spiritually at each Church of God location whenever the local Church of God gathered in person (1 Corinthians 3:16). What is meant by this can surely only be some spiritual and corporate apprehension by the assembled local church of the God who was dwelling among his New Covenant people.

The church is, of course, those believers who have been added together locally in church fellowship, but the Greek word *episunagōgē* is another word that emphasises specific times of actually "assembling" or "meeting together" e.g. in Hebrews 10:25. The original understanding of the "coming together" or "gathering" words in their New Testament church setting in the first century was clearly in terms of the persons concerned coming together by agreed arrangement in time, in space and in common purpose. After this manner, God has designed the local church as people who meet – precisely as had occurred in the past when the tribes congregated at the Jerusalem temple. It doesn't work any other way.

That these New Testament times of church gathering were truly special is underlined in Paul's wording of 1 Corinthians 3:16. He asks, *"Do you not know that you are ... temple of God and that the Spirit of God dwells in you?"* (1 Corinthians 3:16). This verse describes how they were to express their temple identity as a local church of God when they assembled ("came together as a church," en ekklēsia, on the occasions identified in 1 Corinthians 11-14). Other Bible translations make it even plainer that this was a corporate experience of the church once it had gathered. In those translations, the Spirit of God is more emphatically described as dwelling *"among you"* or as dwelling *"in you yourselves"* (NIV), or even dwelling in *"all of you together"* (NLT).

Overall, the Bible teaches that God's House is a holy temple in the Lord (Ephesians 2:22); but then there's the temple identity of a local church (1 Corinthians 3:16) that derives characteristically from that; and finally there's our being indwelt by the Spirit as individual believers (1 Corinthians 6:19).

Do you not know who you are? Paul was asking this of the local church at Corinth. They should have known better (it's one of ten times he uses this corrective technique in 1 Corinthians). The church at Corinth was vulnerable to being destroyed by a foolish Corinthian tendency to split into competitive personality cults by laying claim to different heroes. That was happening among them whenever they gathered, and it was an existential threat to that local fellowship – because anyone causing such division was in danger of destroying the whole local church, and through Paul God warned that he would destroy the person who brought that about.

There's something truly special here in 1 Corinthians 3:16. It's a unique text on the nature and character of local church services. It's perhaps been overlooked or underplayed due to the similarity in wording with a believer's personal indwelling by the Spirit (1 Corinthians 6:19). But by contrast, in 1 Corinthians

6:19 the use of the word "you" is individualistic. This can be seen in the fact that it was used of individuals within the church who could be viewed as consorting with prostitutes, and not used of the whole church corporately. In 1 Corinthians 3:16, however, it is "you" in a corporate sense of all the church. It is "you all" as opposed to "each of you." Both grammar and context makes this plain. And this temple identity is what distinguishes a local church of God from any random gathering of believers of whom it's still true, of course, that they're each personally indwelt by the Spirit of God. This extra and special awareness of the Spirit dwelling corporately among those forming the local church has been taken as arising from the church having come together or assembled as a church.

Biblically, a local church was always connected with its given setting at a particular place. The Church of God established and constituted at a certain place (X) could not operate equally well at other places (Y) or (Z). To that extent, physical location is always relevant when we offer service to God. A biblical church of God has geographical limits; it did not nor cannot operate at any place or function untethered from its given geographical name. That would be a novelty beyond anything found in the Scriptures. The local church is after all "local" – local to some identified place where it was constituted and after which it was named. And so we have, for example, "the church of God which is at Corinth" (1 Corinthians 1:2). The overall temple of God that each biblical local church fits together to form is not every believer, for only local church gatherings that belong to and conform to that temple in character can lay claim to the wonderful insight that 1 Corinthians 3:16 gives us.

The corporate indwelling of the local church by the Spirit of God that we read about there isn't something that we are continually conscious of on a 24/7 basis. We may repeat again at this point what we've rehearsed previously: that God's presence dwelt, for sure, in a specific, localised sense at the Old Testament Temple site right from the time that its construction had been completed. It was always there, but the tribes weren't always there to see or sense it - that's the point. The people weren't there, not until they congregated there on one of the appointed "holy convocations." All the tribes from Dan to Beersheba came together physically at the Place of the Name at three set times of the year annually. There and then only, all the people experienced the Temple-dwelling presence of God that was perpetually localised at the Place of the Name.

The letter to the Hebrews itself makes use of this analogy: it references their *"drawing near"* (e.g. Hebrews 10:1) to God as it refers to those set occasions of the physical gathering of the people. The definite parallel is then explicitly drawn to our attention between Israel's Old Testament *"drawing near"* (in Hebrews 10:1) and the Christian New Testament *"drawing near"* (in Hebrews 10:22, see also 4:16). "Drawing near" as God's people in the New Testament period was by coming together locally as churches and in a spiritual sense both experiencing the corporate aspect of the Spirit's dwelling among us and, as a result of that, expressing the temple character of God's House on earth locally (1 Corinthians 3:16,17).

God dwells in his spiritual Temple or house on a 24/7 basis and each local church of God retains the character of this temple in principle. But – as with the gathering of the

Old Testament tribes – we may conclude that only during the physical assemblings of the local church is God's temple presence to be consciously experienced locally in a corporate way. Those are the very times in biblical language that local churches of God "come together as churches" (en ekklēsia) to function corporately in the way that God in his Word directs that they should. Those biblical church gatherings are when those in the gathered church meet with God, in the sense of having a shared awareness by faith of the divine presence among them through the indwelling Spirit.

Remember the people standing up when Ezra began to read from the Scriptures? The biblical church of God should recognise that, beyond meeting with each other, it is meeting with God at those commanded times of assembling – in the sense of a more acute spiritual apprehension of the God who indwells his spiritual temple 24/7 today!

In summary, we've seen three points converging on one spiritual reality. These are the essence of the word "church" (as when by God's design people meet); but then also the use, and context, of words that further stress the actual times of assembling together to function corporately as God intends; and finally, the striking and common feature of God's people congregating to draw near to God under both covenants. These would all seem to be captured by the wording of 1 Corinthians 14:25, when Paul describes a visitor being found among the assembled church and declaring: *"God is among you."* This isn't satisfied on the individual basis of 1 Corinthians 6, but only on the corporate basis of 1 Corinthians 3.

8

Worshipping in Heaven

The Bible psalmist once prayed that God would open his eyes to see wonderful things from God's Law, that being his Word, the Bible. Now faith doesn't imagine things that are unreal, but only things that may be hidden, at least from some. God has given us his Spirit, the Apostle Paul says in 1 Corinthians 2, so that we may know the things that are freely given to us by God. The chariots of fire that Elisha's servant saw were true spiritual realities. His eyes were opened to see the actual evidence his master had as the basis for his confidence.

The writer of the Hebrews letter was certainly big on drawing parallels with the Old Testament. The rituals of the past are most instructive. That was God's plan all along, of course. The Hebrews' letter talks of the people *"drawing near"* e.g. in chapter 10, verse 1, and that meant drawing near to their God in corporate worship at the Temple. We also know from general background reading of the Old Testament that it was only on set occasions that they did that. And at those times, two things happened: the whole tribal gathering of the people of God experienced God's presence as it was localised at the Temple; but also the High Priest entered into the innermost Holies on one of those days (the Day of Atonement).

Attention switches as we go further down Hebrews chapter 10 to our present day *"drawing near."* This could have begun with nothing other in the first century than New Testament Christians actually coming together in person to function corporately as churches of God. When they did so, they were giving expression to their temple character locally. We've already studied that. But further down still in the same chapter (Hebrews 10), this is followed by the equally stunning disclosure of the spiritual reality we're tracking now in this study: that now all God's people - those gathering together in churches of God - enter the true heavenly Holies in worship. Let's check this out in some more detail.

Chapter 10 of Hebrews begins (see v.1,3 "year by year"; and v.4, "blood of bulls and goats") with the specific Old Testament context being that of one particular annual tribal gathering at the Temple. It's the one known as the Day of Atonement. On this unique day in the year, the high priest entered - hidden from their view - into the innermost part of the Temple where God dwelt on earth among them.

It's probably worth stepping back for a moment into the previous chapter of Hebrews. For it's in Hebrews chapter 9 that we learn something that's most interesting. The early portable Temple, known as the Tabernacle, was comprised of two compartments, an inner and an outer - or, if you like, a first and second section - and these were divided or separated by a veil.

Verses 2&3 and again verses 6&7 define for us the first/outer and the second/inner tabernacle compartments (or tabernacles). Verse 8 goes on to talk about the first/outer compartment being *"still standing."* This wording is only meaningful if (as implied) there should be a time when it would no longer be standing, but rather removed. Indeed v.8 plainly states what is the result of its removal. It makes for the disclosure of the way into the holy place, as signified by the Holy Spirit. The key is v.9a. Here, the ESV Margin sheds more light, saying: *"which is symbolic for the age then present."* The next sentence shows this has to be the meaning; that is, it's a retrospective look back to the time that was then present, back in the Old Testament. Putting it all together, the first/outer tabernacle (while standing) represented symbolically the entire Old Testament economy.

In those days, it was of course a physical impossibility for the congregation to see their high priest enter the copy of the holies (due to the screening provided by that first/outer tabernacle). The Holy Spirit makes capital out of that simple fact. With the coming of Christ (see Hebrews 10:9), the Old Testament economy was taken away or removed to establish the new and living way whereby all God's people get invited into the true holy place in heaven. This is the great disclosure from the Spirit, even the revealing of the way into the Holies. It is a delightful example of visual and conceptual reasoning given by the Lord the Spirit.

By the true sanctuary in heaven is meant the counterpart or answer to the second or inner tabernacle compartment previously on earth, for the one on earth was only a copy modelled on what exists in heaven. This surely teaches us the great and wonderful contrast between then and now, and so between old and new covenant worship by the people of God. But there's more! For, the chapter goes on to tell us more about the ultimate heavenly sanctuary entry we were talking about a moment ago.

But let's first recap that the appointed Old Testament worship ceremonies that form the basis of this great teaching analogy were precisely those occasions when the Old Testament people of God came together to experience the presence of their God that was always localised at the Temple in those days. We remind ourselves that God is indeed everywhere, but the Bible makes it plain that in some special sense his presence was – back then – to be identified in a specific sense with the one place that he himself had chosen out of all their tribal territories. This meant the Tabernacle, and later in turn, at the Temple.

And on one of those times, they assembled, drew near, and watched their representative set off to enter the copy of the heavenly sanctuary that was for them the second section of the Tabernacle or Temple on earth. Under the Old Covenant, there were differing extents to which both people and priests drew near. The people could only go as far as the altar. The priests could access the first compartment of the tabernacle. But it was the high priest, and he alone, who was permitted to enter into the holy place beyond the Tabernacle veil.

But now, in Hebrews chapter 10, comes the amazing revelation, and it's this: following Jesus' death on the cross, all in New Testament churches of God began not only to draw near but to enter the true sanctuary in heaven on a weekly basis (see

Hebrews 10:19; 1 Corinthians 16:2, their giving was when they gathered to break bread; Acts 20:7). Verse 19 of Hebrews chapter 10 gives the explicit invitation to enter the heavenly holy place. Set out for us in sequential detail is the biblical parallel that what corresponded to the tribes of Israel previously having to travel and gather around the Temple, was now the equivalent *"assembling together"* (v.25) in order to *"draw near"* (v.22) and *"enter in"* (v.19) whenever those in New Testament churches of God "came together." And we remember that mention of the particular wording "coming together as a church" (en ekklēsia) only ever occurs in close proximity to the church functions we find being described in 1 Corinthians 11-14. It's in that section of Corinthians that we read about churches breaking bread, gathering for prayer and engaging in the ministry of God's Word. This, then, is the setting for God's people drawing near to God and even entering into his sanctuary that's in heaven above.

We may note in passing that there appears to be close affinity between corporate worship in the Holies and corporate prayers at the Throne of Grace. The prayers of the people of God in Hebrews 4:16 are described using the same wording that's employed for our approach in worship in Hebrews 10:22. Both verses talk about "drawing near." Additionally, ministry of the Word of God when we come together as a church is about being before God, it's about entering his presence, that we might hear from him as his church. While this isn't directly comparable to our entering his presence in worship, again there's a certain similarity.

But let's return to our analogy of what happened under the Old

Covenant and what happens now under the New Covenant. Contrasts are certainly noted, but we can nevertheless compare the similar design features of the people's approach to God in both covenants. This analogy on its own could be thought of as sufficient to prescribe as New Testament teaching the basic idea of a people coming together with each other in order to draw near to their God. But, in addition, we have the unique insight given to us by the text of 1 Corinthians 3:16. That's where we saw the church of God at Corinth being addressed in its temple identity or its temple character, in that it's a local church community conscious of the Spirit of God residing corporately among them. As churches of God were part of a whole community forming a holy temple for God, the quality or character of the whole extended to each part. Tensions in their church fellowship at Corinth threatened this and the letter Paul wrote to them was in large part an urgent appeal to church unity.

On all such occasions where and when the local Church of God gathers in person, it's to be spiritually aware that the Temple-dwelling presence of God is to be experienced by faith at its given geographical location. At all times when we "come together as a church" (1 Corinthians 11-14) by assembling locally, we are by faith (in what God's Word teaches) to experience in a corporate way a spiritual apprehension of God dwelling among us by his Spirit (1 Corinthians 3:16).

The clear indication is that it's this gathering that in turn facilitates our spiritual entry among all of God's people into the holy place in heaven. When we get to verse 19 of Hebrews chapter 10, this is made explicit: *"Therefore, brothers and sisters, since we have confidence to enter the holy place by the blood of Jesus"* (Hebrews 10:19).

After the opening verses setting up the lesson taught by the Old Testament, it's in the flow of Hebrews 10 that we come to this current invitation for all followers of Christ's teaching through his Apostles: it's an invitation for corporate worship that accesses the spiritual realm in the heavenly and true tabernacle that the Lord himself pitched and not Moses. While we may infer the assembling of believers forming the local church is the means by which we draw near and participate in this spiritual reality, Hebrews chapter 10 goes further and vigorously promotes the physical assembling of New Testament churches in verse 25: *"Let's consider how to encourage one another in love and good deeds, not abandoning our own meeting together, as is the habit of some people, but encouraging one another"* (Hebrews 10:24-25).

The meaning becomes all the more obvious now, that it's the gathering of those persons who in essence are the church, when assembled in one place with a single purpose to carry out its duties, that brings about its sanctuary experience. Why? Because Hebrews 10 progresses from the Old Testament drawing near in corporate worship to mention New Testament drawing near in corporate worship, and then onto God's priesthood on earth entering the holy place in heaven (vv.19-23, the "hope" of entering in), before in the same immediate context exhorting the persons who enter in above not to forsake their physical gathering on earth below (vv.24,25). Following the flow of the context of the Hebrews chapter 10 text like this we can see spiritual worship in heaven being implemented or facilitated through physical gathering on earth.

What's more, this understanding of Hebrews 10 agrees with 1 Peter 2:5 where we were earlier introduced to the idea of gathering on earth so that we might enter into heaven: *"coming to Him* [or drawing near to Him] *as to a living stone which has been rejected by people, but is choice and precious in the sight of God, you also, as living stones, are being built up as a spiritual house for a holy priesthood, to offer spiritual sacrifices"* (1 Peter 2:4-5).

A local church can only function by gathering for, as we said before, the essence of the word "church" is found in the gathering of disciples to worship God. Of course, we come to Christ for salvation on an individual basis, but the coming Peter talks about is of obedient believers drawing near as gathered worshippers (on earth) to function as temple priests – as a priestly house, in fact, for the offering up of spiritual sacrifices (in heaven). The *"drawing near"* to Christ in this verse is again directly comparable with the same kind of *"drawing near"* when the gathered tribes of Israelite worshippers came to the temple three times each year.

And notice this: we draw near to Christ, the Living Stone (v.4) and where is he? He's the precious Cornerstone of God's House on earth that has been laid in Zion in heaven (v.6). We said the verse is dealing with God's design for Christian worship for it talks of a holy priesthood offering up spiritual sacrifices of praise. Living stones on earth drawing near to the Living Stone in heaven. This would once again indicate that the drawing near of the gathered people activates an experience that is simultaneously one that occurs in two places at one time. There is the gathering of the priestly house on earth for the purpose of drawing near to offer spiritual sacrifices and where we draw near to is the very sanctuary in heavenly Zion above where Christ is, exalted as the primary Living Stone and Cornerstone in God's House.

We remember how Jesus, in John chapter 4 (vv.21-24), said Christian worship today would be no longer material, but rather spiritual in nature – no longer shadowy, but the true substance. It's both true to say that our service is "not earthbound" AND that physical entailments remain as we operate from "different places geographically." Spiritual entities replace the items listed for God's Old Covenant people (in Exodus 19:5,6). And though in many different local churches globally, we enter as a united people into a spiritual sanctuary that's not of this world (Hebrews 9). This is the eye-opening spiritual reality of what it means to be a gathered priesthood worshipping in heaven (see Hebrews 3:6; 6:19; 10:19)!

About Hayes Press

Hayes Press (www.hayespress.org) is a registered charity in the United Kingdom, whose primary mission is to disseminate the Word of God. It is one of the largest distributors of gospel tracts and leaflets in the United Kingdom, with over 100 titles and many thousands dispatched annually. In addition to paperbacks and eBooks, Hayes Press also publishes Plus Eagles' Wings, a fun and educational Bible magazine for children, and Golden Bells, a popular daily Bible reading calendar.

If you would like to contact Hayes Press, there are a number of ways you can do so:

By mail: c/o The Barn, Flaxlands, Royal Wootton Bassett, Wiltshire, UK SN4 8DY

By phone: 01793 850598

By eMail: info@hayespress.org

via Facebook: www.facebook.com/hayespress.org

About the Author

Born and educated in Scotland, Brian worked as a government scientist until God called him into full-time Christian ministry on behalf of the Churches of God (www.churchesofgod.info). His voice has been heard on Search For Truth radio broadcasts for over 40 years (visit www.searchfortruth.podbean.com) during which time he has been an itinerant Bible teacher throughout the UK. His evangelical and missionary work outside the UK is primarily in Belgium, The Philippines and South East Central Africa. He is married to Rosemary, with a son and daughter.

You can connect with me on:

https://www.amazon.com/stores/Brian-Johnston/author/B00NPJFXZU

Also by Brian Johnston

The Tabernacle - God's House of Shadows

Why did God go into such great detail with Moses as to exactly how the Tabernacle was to be built and the offerings that were to be made there? And why did He include it all in our Bibles? Is it just rather dry, ancient history or is there anything that is applicable to Christians today – thousands of years later?

Brian provides insights into a subject that many find daunting - including how components of the Tabernacle provide very relevant pictures of the service that God expects from Christians today.

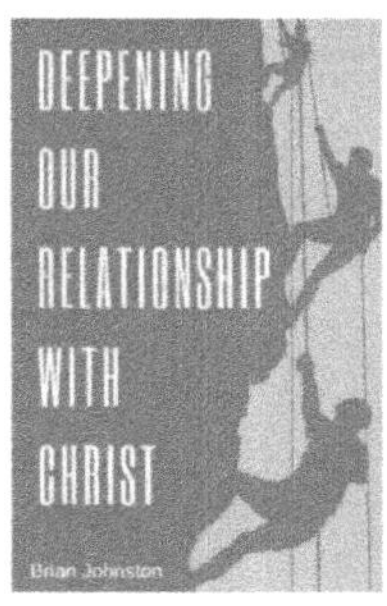

Deepening Our Relationship with Christ

The first step in our relationship with Jesus is accepting Him as our Saviour - but that's just the beginning! In this short book, Brian expounds 8 important ways that every Christian should deepen their personal relationship with Christ: (1) in being in union with Him, (2) in being built on Him, (3) in being United by and with Him, (4) in following Him, (5) in owning Him as Head of the Body, (6) in being added alongside Him, (7) in being subject to Him as Son over God's House, (8) in remembering Him.

Living in God's House

God uses the analogy of a garden to illustrate that He doesn't want Christians to be isolated after they've been born again. Like a gardener, He wants to gather and plant them together in an organised garden setting. Likewise, God is a builder that brings individual stones together to form His house according to His own design. In this book, Brian traces the development of God's House in the Bible and how it can still function today.